MODELING AND SIMULATION OF HUMAN BEHAVIOR

AN INTRODUCTION

EMORY SANDERS

MODELING AND SIMULATION OF HUMAN BEHAVIOR
AN INTRODUCTION

iUniverse books may be ordered through booksellers or by contacting:

iUniverse
1663 Liberty Drive
Bloomington, IN 47403
www.iuniverse.com
844-349-9409

ISBN: 978-1-6632-3022-5 (sc)
ISBN: 978-1-6632-3023-2 (e)

Library of Congress Control Number: 2021923399

Print information available on the last page.

iUniverse rev. date: 11/24/2021

TABLE OF CONTENTS

FOREWORD

A review of current models to simulate human behavior shows that many models were developed to identify behavioral determinants and processes that are part of man-environment interactions associated with specific applications such as use of resources, policy strategies, and social applications (e.g. Jager & Mosler, 2007, Cialdini & Goldstein, 2004, and Mosler & Brucks, 2003).

Although the current models represent valuable tools for specific situations, it was necessary to develop a general model that is based on behavioral and social concepts to simulate human behavior. This is the purpose of the current work presented in this book. The behavior model developed is based on personal behavior determinants represented mathematically by a vector whose magnitude and direction simulates the forces exerted on the individual and the goal of the individual, respectively. The proposed model was extended to a group of individuals.

The model developed is needed in the field of behavior modeling and simulation as it

(1) allows to model and simulate behavior comprehensively by taking into account factors, forces, and values that influence behavior
(2) accounts for the role of past experience and resources that the individual can use
(3) allows to model and simulate behavior through a logical decision process
(4) accounts for risk due to uncertainties in the behavioral model and the decision process

Although the basis of the behavioral model relies on theoretical concepts, the proposed model presents many practical applications particularly in the areas of

- inter-relationship between factors, forces, and values that influence personal and group behavior
- processing of past experience
- simulation of the decision process
- risk associated with uncertainties

This book was primarily written for

(1) psychology and sociology professionals to provide a comprehensive reference work on behavior modeling and simulation
(2) computer scientists and simulation professionals with an interest in human behavior modeling and simulation
(3) individuals involved in decision making and who need guidance through their decision process. The decisions involved may be a relatively simple task (such as buying a house) or a more elaborate process (such as getting married or getting a divorce)
(4) groups of individuals involved in decision making and who need guidance through their decision process. The decisions involved may be a relatively simple task (such as creating and operating a legal organization) or a more elaborate process (such as creating and operating an academic organization)
(5) individuals or groups of individuals with an interest in human behavior modeling and simulation or decision analysis

Although special care was provided to describe the processes involved in modeling and simulation of human behavior, readers are encouraged to consult the applicable flowcharts presented in the book to obtain maximum clarity on the processes and their inter-relationships. Summary Tables have also been provided to summarize model applications to specific purposes and situations.

1.0 INTRODUCTION

Understanding human behavior is generally a difficult task because of the complexity of the individual (or the group of individuals) that is subjected to intertwined factors, forces, values, and other motivational resources that are influencing behavior.

A preliminary qualitative model of the individual in life is developed to account for the factors and forces exerted on the individual and the individual's goals (Chapter 2).

Personal behavior is further modeled mathematically and represented by a vector with two important characteristics that are magnitude and direction (Chapter 3). The magnitude of the behavior vector depends on the factors and forces exerted that may be unleveraged or leveraged. The direction of the behavior vector includes the goals and purposes of the individual.

The behavior model was extended to a group of individuals (Chapter 4). The group vector is characterized by a predefined direction that encompasses the common goals of the group members and a magnitude that includes the values, forces, and other factors that are important to the group's mission. The group vector model also includes special cases that are the homogeneous group vector, the heterogeneous group vector, cases characterized by the absence of magnitude and direction, and other cases related to the group's internal and external relations.

The description of the basic human behavior model is provided (Chapter 5) and includes the various factors and values exerted on the individual to behave in a task-oriented or relationship-oriented environment, or a combination of both. The relevant factors identified include varying factors, immutable factors, values, factors related to self-interest, and human limitations.

The forces exerted on the individual are numerous and have been identified as the forces impacting the individual behavior vector. These forces are the unleveraged and leveraged forces (Chapter 6). A description of the effects of these forces is provided. Representative factors affecting the individual's behavior are listed.

Similarly, the forces and factors exerted and impacting the group of individual's behavior are described (Chapter 7). Representative factors affecting the group's behavior are listed.

The role of past experience on the individual's behavior is described in Chapter 8.0. Five steps have been identified to process past experience and include knowledge of the facts, analysis, learning, judgment, and interpretation.

The resources supporting and influencing the individual's behavior to achieve his or her goals are part of the human behavior model. These resources are the unleveraged and leveraged resources and are discussed in Chapter 9.0.

Similarly, the resources supporting and influencing the group of individuals in their behavior have been identified and are discussed in Chapter 10.0. Some of these resources include inherent qualities related to the group members, as well as internal and external resources.

The decision process for the individual and the group is described in Chapter 11.0. This process is intimately related to human behavior since it is mostly through decisions that behavior is developed and adopted so that individuals and groups can act appropriately to achieve their goals. The decision process includes two stages where in the first stage an initial decision is reached and is followed by a second stage where uncertainties are resolved to lead to a final decision.

The human behavior model also includes immutable factors to guide the individual towards a task-oriented or relationship-oriented human behavior. The immutable elements of success are presented and discussed in Chapter 12.0.

The error process is related to the decision process of the individual and the group that may include unresolved uncertainties (Chapter 11.0). The error process described in Chapter 13.0 allows to identify and correct errors so that the decision taken is accurate, complete, and up to date.

A risk analysis is presented in Chapter 14.0 where risk is analyzed as it relates to

(1) the individual and group behavior due to uncertainties
(2) the decision process where uncertainties may create a risk in the final decision adopted for behavior and action toward goals

Several illustrative applications of the human behavior model are presented and discussed in Chapter 15.0. These applications relate to the individual and the group decision process methodologies. Furthermore, lists are provided describing examples of applications of the individual and group decision process methodologies as they are applied to specific purposes and situations.

Specific extensions of the human behavior model are presented and discussed (Section 15.2). Some noteworthy extensions include the vector representation, the impact of self-interest on human behavior, the error process, the need for computer simulation in the behavior model, the risk methodology, and the validation of the model.

Conclusions derived from the vector-based human behavior model for the individual and the group are provided in Chapter 16.0.

2.0 THE INDIVIDUAL BEHAVIOR MODEL

The model of the individual behavior is based on the individual submitted to factors affecting his or her behavior and to forces exerted on the individual.

The factors may be varying factors such as technological, material, economic, and social, or immutable factors such as the individual personality, character, values, and principles.

The forces on the individual are categorized into two types:

(1) Unleveraged forces on which the individual has no or very little control. Examples of such forces are governmental, legal, and natural forces.
(2) Leveraged forces on which the individual has full or partial control. Examples of such forces are professional, religious, and technological.

The combination of the factors and forces act directly on the individual to influence and allow him or her to focus and act on his or her purposes and goals. The purposes and goals may be material, spiritual, professional, family-oriented, or any other goals targeted by the individual. Fulfillment of these purposes and goals represents the individual's accomplishments.

The model also assumes that the individual is subjected to factors and forces that are part of a national legal system where the civil rights and liberties of the individual (or group of individuals) are respected and protected by laws. The model does not consider any form of coercion or illegal act, factor, or force exerted on the individual to influence his or her endeavor.

The above assumption will be used in all aspects of the individual (or group of individuals) behavior model.

The model of the individual submitted to factors and forces and targeting purpose and goals is shown schematically in Fig. 1.

As an example, an individual who wishes to apply for a job or change job will face the unleveraged forces of the job market, the timing of the job change, and the status of the economy. The leveraged forces exerted on the individual may be his or her education level, professional experience, and family-exerted pressure.

3.0 THE INDIVIDUAL BEHAVIOR AS A VECTOR

After defining the factors and forces that influence the individual's behavior, it is important to define the tool to be used to represent behavior. This Chapter addresses the issue of behavior representation.

The individual is assumed to be responsible and in control of his or her own behavior. As such, personal behavior is modeled and represented by a vector with two main characteristics: magnitude and direction.

The magnitude of the vector is impacted by the forces and factors described in Chapter 2.0. The forces mostly controlled by the individual are the leveraged forces such as the individual's values, resources, experience, and limitations. The unleveraged forces, however, impact the individual's behavior but are not controlled by the individual. Examples of such forces are political, social, legal, and natural forces.

The direction of the behavior vector includes the goals and purposes set by the individual.

The representation of the individual behavior vector is shown schematically in Fig. 2(a).

The example of the individual who wishes to apply for a job or change job presented in Chapter 2.0 is an example of vectorial behavior representation. In addition to the forces exerted on the individual, there may be his or her own experience, the resources available (such as networking, etc.), limitations (such as time, financial constraints, etc.), and other relevant factors (such as economic and social factors, etc.).

There are two particular cases related to human behavior represented by a vector:

- Case 1: The vector has no magnitude. This case indicates an individual behavior that has a direction that cannot be applied through an inner magnitude, or factor. In practical terms, this individual behavior results in no action towards a purpose or a goal. The remedy for this deficiency is to seek strength and resources to be provided to the individual.

- Case 2: The vector has no direction. This case shows an individual behavior that has forces and factors applied with no coherence and consistency towards a purpose or a goal, resulting in no action. The remedy for this deficiency is to provide the individual with intelligence and data to create a purpose and goal for the individual to reach.

4.0 THE GROUP BEHAVIOR AS A VECTOR

The vector representation is now extended to the representation of a group of individuals.

The behavior of a group of individuals is more complex than the behavior of a single individual as the group members must adhere to specific characteristics and standards that were defined for the group in order to achieve the group's specific purposes and goals.

The group vector includes

- a pre-defined direction that encompasses the common goals and aspirations of the group members.
- a magnitude that is common to all group members that reflects the strength and forces applied by the group members in order to achieve their purposes and goals.

The group members are generally subjected to a screening process prior to joining the group

- through indoctrination and education according to a specific set of procedures and rules so that each group member fully understands the group purposes and goals.

- through training in order to fully identify themselves with the group.

The screening process also serves to identify the group members who are "rejects" because they cannot belong to the group: they cannot align their individual vector with the standard group vector with respect to direction and/or magnitude. The rejects may include dissidents, outsiders, inept or unfit individuals, underperformers, and non-desirable individuals.

The group standards are used to sustain the group vector in both direction and magnitude and include:

-   The group moral and ethical values
-   The factors that influence the group behavior
-   The forces exerted on the group members
-   The experience of the group members
-   The resources required from the group members
-   The synergy expected to be achieved by the group members common behavior
-   The common behavior expected from each group member.
-   The limitations of the group members with respect to focus on the goals and capabilities

The representation of the group behavior vector is shown schematically in Fig. 2(b).

As an example of group vectorial representation, a group of individuals may wish to create and operate a legal organization. The leveraged forces exerted on the group may be the group's mission, and level of education, profession, training, and financial status of the group members. The unleveraged forces exerted on the group may be the timing of the operation and the political, social, and legal forces expected to be exerted on the group. The group may be submitted to internal forces (through management of the group), external forces (through external influence and control), and relations with other groups (through affiliations and/or partnership). All these forces must be taken into consideration as the group makes the decision to create and operate a legal organization.

An example of the screening process would be to have strict requirements for all applicants wishing to join a legal organization involved in legal and civil rights. These requirements might be as follows:

Education required: Law degree

Professional experience: 5 years as a trial lawyer

Association: member of an accredited bar association

Current practice of law: Active

Specialty: Civil rights law, criminal law

Experience: demonstrated experience in civil rights, voting rights, religious liberties, First Amendment, or employment and housing discrimination

The above requirements define the group standard behavior vector (in both direction and magnitude) for admission into the group.

Ultimately, all individual's behavior vectors need to be aligned with the standard group behavior vector for optimal group behavior.

4.1 VECTORIAL OPERATIONS

The vectorial operations considered in the resulting behavior vector of the group are limited to addition and subtraction for the sake of simplicity.

Addition of the magnitude components of the behavior vectors of individual members will result in an increase in the magnitude of the group behavior vector, therefore providing added forces, factors, and synergy to the group vector to reach the group goals.

However, the increase in magnitude of the group vector, and thus the added synergy, will only be achieved if the group members behavior vectors have the same direction. If the group members behavior vectors are not aligned in the same direction, no benefit of synergy will result.

Subtraction of the magnitude components of the behavior vectors of individual members will result in a reduction in the magnitude of the group behavior vector, particularly for negative factors and forces, possibly reducing the group behavior disadvantages and shortfalls.

The subtraction, however, will only be beneficial to the group behavior if the group member behavior vectors are aligned in the same direction.

A typical example of vectorial operation is related to the individual behavior vectors of two individuals who wish to marry and/or live together. A vector evaluation based on addition and/or subtraction operation allows to determine if the union of the two individuals can result in a compatible and harmonious relationship. This example is discussed in further detail in Chapter 15.1.

4.2 HOMOGENEOUS GROUP VECTOR

There are groups of individuals and associations where the individual vectors are fully aligned with the group vector: this is the case of the homogeneous vector.

The advantage of this group is that the group direction and magnitude are never challenged. There is no dissent. The group behavior is expected uniformly through the prescribed rules and authority of the group leader. The group will function smoothly to accomplish its goals. Risk of such a group, however, is related to the "think tank" as there is no criticism or opposition to the group leadership.

Examples of homogeneous groups are professional associations, military groups, and some political groups.

4.3 HETEROGENOUS GROUP VECTOR

There are groups and associations where the individual vectors need not be fully aligned with the group vector: this is the case of the heterogeneous vector.

The advantages of this group are that individuals are not coerced into a "group think". Differences of opinions and dissent are allowed. The group functions smoothly because the differences between the group members behavior are tolerated.

The risks of such a group are that differences of behavior between group members may lead to the group malfunction, fighting between members, or paralysis.

Examples of heterogeneous groups are some professional associations and liberal political parties.

4.4 PARTICULAR CASES:

Particular situations with the group vector representation are examined through the following cases:

Case 1: The group vector is without magnitude. This case indicates a group that lacks strength and resources to be applied towards its goals. This group behavior results in no action towards the group goals.

Case 2: The group vector is without direction. This case shows a group behavior that has exerted forces and factors, strength, and resources but the group lacks focus and leadership to achieve its goals. Ultimately, this group behavior becomes erratic with no specific purpose.

It is therefore clear from the two above cases that a proper balance of magnitude and direction needs to be achieved in order to reach an optimum group behavior that is well supported by the strength and resources and that is targeted towards clearly defined goals.

Case 3: Internal threats

The group leadership must identify and mitigate (or eliminate) internal threats "from within" to retain its strengths and resources and stay focused towards its goals. The vectors of the group members must remain aligned with the group vectors both in direction and magnitude at all times.

Case 4: External relations and threats

The group leadership must build and maintain good relations with external groups and organizations with understanding and collaboration based on mutual benefits. This also helps create synergy. The group behavior vector must therefore be aligned with the external collaborating groups. However, external threat from other group vectors (both in magnitude and direction) must be identified and thwarted to avoid detrimental situations to the group.

5.0 THE HUMAN BEHAVIOR MODEL

The human behavior model is based on the fact that various factors and values are exerted and influence the individual to behave in a task-oriented or relationship-oriented environment, or a combination of both.

The factors are

(1) Varying factors that vary with circumstances and time. Examples of these factors are material, technological, economic, or social factors.

(2) Immutable factors that are proper to the individual and that are not prone to change. Examples of these factors are the individual's personality and character. Other immutable factors are factors that have been acquired with time by the individual and that may include the individual's inner values and principles.

(3) Factors related to the individual's short- and/or long-term self-interest that will force the individual to adopt a certain behavior.

(4) The limitations relevant to the individual's proper behavior. Such limitations may be physical, mental, intellectual, or social.

The human behavior model is shown schematically in Fig. 3.

The example of the individual who wishes to apply for a job or change job presented in Chapter 2.0 is a typical example of the human behavior model. The individual is submitted to varying factors (such as material, economic, social, etc.), immutable factors (such as personality, character, etc.), inner values and principles, and limitations (such as temporal and financial constraints, etc.) that will influence the individual's behavior in a task-oriented environment.

6.0 FORCES AND FACTORS ON THE INDIVIDUAL

6.1 FORCES EXERTED ON THE INDIVIDUAL

The forces exerted on the individual are numerous and have been identified as influencing the individual behavior vector both in direction and magnitude. The forces are categorized as:

(1) Unleveraged forces. These forces are exerted on the individual regardless of the individual's will and interests. The forces have been imposed on the individual and the resulting individual's behavior must be in full compliance with the requirements of these forces. Ignoring these forces or failure to comply will lead to adverse consequences or sanctions imposed on the individual.

Examples of unleveraged forces are forces imposed by time (such as deadlines), governmental and legal forces (such as laws), natural forces, and economic and financial forces.

(2) Leveraged forces. These forces are due to the individual's will and choice and may be part of his or her professional, educational, technological, or religious background. These forces may also be due to the individual's inner values, family-exerted influence, peer-pressure, or self-interest.

It is therefore a combination of the unleveraged and leveraged forces exerted on the individual that will yield a resulting individual behavior vector with a specific direction and magnitude.

The unleveraged and leveraged forces exerted on the individual are shown in Fig. 4(a). Examples of forces exerted on the individual are also summarized in Table 1.

6.2 EFFECTS OF THE UNLEVERAGED FORCES ON THE INDIVIDUAL

The effects of the unleveraged forces on the individual are due to

(1) Man-made forces such as governmental, political, social, and legal forces that require the individual to behave in a prescribed way. Failure to follow the rules of conduct may result in violation of the law or regulation, and may lead to punitive sanctions against the individual.

An example of a man-made force may be the requirement for every individual to pay taxes. Ignoring this requirement will result in violation of the tax law and will make the individual liable.

(2) Natural forces such as the forces of nature, time, and the environment that are immutable and overwhelm the individual in his or her behavior. In this case, the individual must totally submit to the natural forces. There is no alternative.

An example of natural force may be the health status of the individual. An individual in poor health will be restricted and therefore may not behave in ways that will be detrimental to his health.

Examples of the effects of unleveraged forces exerted on the individual are shown in Table 2(a).

6.3 EFFECTS OF THE LEVERAGED FORCES ON THE INDIVIDUAL

The effects of the leveraged forces on the individual are complex since they may be due to various sources that have a significant impact on the individual's behavior. These forces have also been selected and felt by the individual in their proper directions and magnitudes. The result is a mixture of leveraged forces that the individual will follow as his or her principles and will be part of the foundation of his or her behavior.

An example of leverage force may be the moral values that an individual uses in all aspects of his or her behavior.

Self-interest also represents a leveraged force that is essentially concentrated only on the individual's self for his or her own benefit. Self-interest may be for the short-term or long-term goals of the individual and may be fully or partially known to the individual. The self-interest force may be intense and may overwhelm all other forces in influencing the individual's behavior.

Examples of the effects of leveraged forces exerted on the individual are shown in Table 2(b).

6.4 FACTORS AFFECTING THE INDIVIDUAL'S BEHAVIOR

Examples of factors affecting the individual's behavior are shown in Table 3(a). These factors include mostly laws, specific requirements on the individual, and factors affecting personal values.

An example of factor affecting the individual's behavior is the professional code of ethics of an organization that the individual wishes to join.

7.0 FORCES AND FACTORS ON THE GROUP

7.1 FORCES EXERTED ON THE GROUP

The forces exerted on the group are based on the unleveraged and leverages forces exerted on the individual (Fig. 4(a)). Some major differences exist, however, as the group behavior is more prone to conceptual forces involving ideology and doctrine, training of the group members, and "groupthink" effect. Other differences may include internal and external forces exerted on the group, and forces stemming from relations with other groups.

The group's specific forces are examined below:

The force of ideology and doctrine on the group is extremely powerful when present in the group. The force relies on principles set to justify the existence and cohesiveness of the group and guide the group through its growth and perpetuation. The direction and magnitude of the group behavior vector are well defined, and any deviation from the goals set are avoided at all costs. Training of the group members is essential for maintaining the group's standard behavior. Policy and procedures are developed and implemented to that effect to support and guide the group members.

The effect of the "groupthink" stems from an internal force exerted by the group leaders over time to force the group members to adopt a preset pattern of thought and behavior characterized by forced consent and conformity to the group values and purposes.

Internal forces on the group are due to the management of the group and include forces related to planning, organization, control, and the leadership of the group itself. The leadership of the group can make a significant difference since it may encourage open discussion and self-criticism regarding the group's behavior, or it may not tolerate any form of criticism and dissent.

External forces on the group are related to the influence, review, and control that other organizations may have on the group. Relations with other groups, affiliations, and common interests with external entities may impact the group's behavior and structure. As a result, the group may experience expansion or contraction.

Self-interest represents a leveraged force that is essentially concentrated on the group's self for its own benefit. Self-interest may be for the short-term or long-term benefit of the group members and may be fully or partially known to the group members or may be known only to the group leaders.

The group self-interest force may be the dominant force of the group's behavior if the group's ideology, values, or very existence are threatened.

It must be noted that the group's goals and policy may be revised as needed to adjust the group's behavior to varying conditions or situations. If no revisions or amendments are needed, the group will strive to perpetuate its ideology and behavior.

The forces exerted on the group are shown in Fig. 4(b).

7.2 FACTORS AFFECTING THE GROUP'S BEHAVIOR

Examples of factors affecting the group's behavior are shown in Table 3(b). These factors include mostly laws, specific requirements on the group, and internal and external factors.

As an example, the behavior of a professional organization will be affected by existing professional laws and required level of education and training of its members.

8.0 PAST EXPERIENCE

Past experience refers to the human behavior model presented in chapter 5.0 where it was shown that varying factors, immutable factors, values and principles, and self-interest are exerted on the individual and influence him or her to behave in a task-oriented or relationship-oriented environment.

In this chapter, the role of past experience is reviewed as being an important resource to help the individual adopt a behavior to achieve his or her goals.

Past experience impacts the individual behavior vector mostly in its magnitude, although in some cases it may have an influence on the individual's goals.

Past experience can be broken up into five steps that allow to dissect the various stages of the experience at hand and examine the options available to process the experience. The five steps of past experience are:

(1) Know the facts. This step allows to gather the relevant facts and data available.
(2) Analyze the facts and data for their validity, accuracy, and completeness. An important task is also to make sure that the individual knows what he or she knows, and that the individual knows what he or she does not know.
(3) Learn from the experience and assess the nature of the experience (good or bad).
(4) Judge the facts of the experience through discernment.
(5) Interpret the experience and its results through explanation and understanding.

The results of past experience are either to

(1) Acknowledge, accept, remember, and store the experience as having an impact on behavior and, if needed, change that behavior.
(2) Ignore, deny, and forget the experience as having no impact on behavior.

The role of past experience is shown in Fig. 5.

9.0 RESOURCES SUPPORTING THE INDIVIDUAL

The resources supporting and influencing the individual behavior in order to achieve the set goals are part of the human behavior model described in Chapter 5.

The resources are categorized as

(1) Unleveraged resources that the individual can use regardless of the individual's will or past experience. These resources have been given naturally to the individual or have been naturally developed by the individual over time. The resources include natural and health resources, genetics, character, personality, and other internal resources acquired naturally by the individual.

(2) Leveraged resources that the individual has acquired willfully through his own experience and judgment over time. These resources are part of the individual's values acquired in his or her environment and the individual may use them at will to achieve his or her goals.

These resources were selected and retained by the individual and include values, ethics, and principles as they relate to education, profession, religion, social environment, and other external resources.

Representative resources supporting the individual are listed in Table 4.

10.0 RESOURCES SUPPORTING THE GROUP

The resources supporting and influencing the group in their behavior in order to achieve the group goals are based on the human behavior model (Chapter 5) and some of the forces exerted on the group (Chapter 7).

The resources are categorized as

(1) Unleveraged resources that include inner natural resources of the group members, their characters, personalities, and values. Other resources include the unleveraged ties to social and political networks, as well as legal and financial resources.

(2) Leveraged resources that the group has acquired willfully through operation and experience over time. Such resources may include inherent qualities related to the group members (such as education, profession, experience, religion, ethics, values, principles, etc.), indoctrination, and training.

Leverage resources also include internal resources proper to the group (such as group structure, organization, leadership, and control) and external resources (such as affiliations with other groups). Also included as leveraged resources are financial resources and fundraising, group membership, and policy.

Representative resources supporting the group are listed in Table 5.

11.0 THE DECISION PROCESS

The decision process model assumes that the decision process is intimately related to human behavior since it is through decisions that behavior is developed and adopted so that the individual or the group of individuals can act appropriately to achieve their goals. This assumption is consistent with other model assumptions (e.g. Jager & Mosler, 2007). Other motivational processes based on people's needs (e.g. Maslow, 1954, Max-Neef, 1992) and social processes (Rogers, 1995, and Delre, Jager, Janssen, 2006) have been reported but will not be considered in the current model for the sake of simplicity.

11.1 THE INDIVIDUAL DECISION PROCESS

The individual decision process includes two distinct stages that yield an initial and a final decision.

In the first stage, knowledge, facts, and factors are initially gathered and analyzed by the individual using his or her own internal and external resources. The impact of the initial decision to be taken is analyzed versus leveraged and unleveraged forces and other constraints to uphold the initial decision.

The second stage includes the identification and resolution of uncertainties present in the initial decision. This is followed by researching and resolving the outcomes of "what-if" scenarios. The decision is then reviewed by the individual to determine if the decision is in his or her best interest. This stage ends with the acceptance of a final decision so that the proper personal behavior can be adopted (after adjustment, if needed) and allow the individual to act toward his or her goals.

The individual decision process is shown schematically in Fig. 6.

Table 6 provides a list of examples of individual decision processes as they are applied to specific purposes and situations. The list includes representative examples and may be extended or updated.

As an example, let us assume that an individual wants to decide if he or she should make an investment in a particular company.

In the first stage, the individual will gather and analyze data, facts, and factors on the company using his or her own internal and external resources. The individual will analyze the initial decision to be made versus leveraged and unleveraged forces and constraints (see Fig. 4(a)) to uphold the initial decision. The leveraged forces may be the knowledge and investment proficiency of the individual. The unleveraged forces may be the status of the economy, interest rates, and market conditions. The constraints may be the amount of money available to invest and the expected return on investment (ROI).

The second stage includes the resolution of uncertainties present in the initial decision and the consideration and resolution of "what-if" scenarios. The uncertainties may be related to the profitability of the company, its expected earnings, and any factors affecting its growth. This stage ends with the acceptance of the final decision so that the individual can adopt the proper personal behavior and act toward his or her goal to make the investment.

11.2 THE GROUP DECISION PROCESS

The group decision process is similar to the individual decision process in the initial stage. Knowledge, facts, and factors are gathered and analyzed by the group members using internal and external resources. The impact of the initial decision is then determined versus leveraged and unleveraged forces and constraints to uphold the initial decision. The major differences, however, is that the group will need to create subgroups and committees for the review and processing of the initial decision. This is due to the nature of the group decision process that generally includes high stakes and far-reaching consequences.

As the initial decision is reached, the second stage includes the identification and resolution of the uncertainties and "what-if" scenarios by the different subgroups so that the decision can be recommended to the group. The decision is then reviewed by the group members and submitted to a vote. Appropriate revisions and amendments are made until the final decision is adopted and voted by the group.

The group then develops a policy for the implementation of the decision. The group members and leaders are responsible for their decision and will act towards achieving the goals of the group.

The group decision process is shown in Fig. 7.

Table 7 provides a list of examples of group decision processes as they are applied to specific purposes and situations. The list includes representative examples and may be extended or updated.

As an example, let us assume that a group of individuals wants to decide if it should create and operate a professional association.

In the first stage, the group (or subgroup) members will gather and analyze data, facts, and factors on the planned professional association using internal and external resources. The group will analyze the initial decision to be made by identifying components of the decision and creating subgroups and committees, as needed, to review the initial decision. The different review groups will analyze the initial decision versus leveraged and unleveraged forces, and constraints (see Fig. 4(b)) to uphold the initial decision. The leveraged forces may be the professional association ideology, level of education, professional aptitude, and code of ethics. The unleveraged forces may be the political and social environment, and the legal requirements for creating and operating such an association.

The constraints may be the financial soundness of the association, its management structure, and its support from the industry. Other decision considerations may include the internal structure of the association, the external forces expected to be exerted on the association, and the relations and possible affiliations with other associations.

The second stage includes the resolution of uncertainties present in the initial decision and the resolution of "what-if" scenarios. The uncertainties may be related to the expected membership of the association, the benefits provided to members, the political support provided to the association, and the recognition or accreditation of the association.

The second stage ends with the vote and the adoption of the final decision so that the group can adopt the proper behavior and act toward its goal to create and operate a professional association.

11.3 RESOLUTION OF UNCERTAINTIES

The individual and group decision processes include an important step where uncertainties must be identified and resolved. This step is followed by the resolutions of "what-if" scenarios (Figs. 6 and 7).

As seen, the major sources of uncertainties in the decision process are

- The facts
- The factors
- The limitations
- Self-interest
- Internal resources
- External resources
- Leveraged forces
- Constraints

Note that the above uncertainties do not include the unleveraged forces that are exerted on the individual or the group regardless of any other factors or forces. The unleveraged forces are assumed to include no uncertainties.

The methodology for resolving uncertainties consists of varying (or eliminating) the magnitude of the uncertainties in the decision process and analyzing the impact on the decision. Although this variational process is qualitative and iterative, the sources of uncertainties can be narrowed to the important uncertainties identified in the following: the major factors, the strictest limitations, the important uncertainties that could be driving self-interest, uncertainties in the major resources used by the decision maker, influential leveraged forces, and the uncertainties in the most significant constraints.

This process results in the identification of the important uncertainties in the decision process.

The final step consists of using the uncertainties identified in the decision process to yield a reasonably conservative scenario; hence, a conservative decision will be used for the individual and the group.

It must be noted that the level of conservatism in the decision reached by the individual and the group depends on the conservatism used in the uncertainties in the decision-making process and ultimately depends on the judgment of the decision maker.

Following the example of Chapter 11.1, the resolution of uncertainties for the individual decision process would be to consider investing in the company by varying the profitability of the company while keeping all other sources of uncertainty constant. The individual would then be able to determine a reasonably conservative level of profitability of the company to allow him or her to invest.

The above process would be repeated by varying the expected earnings of the company, while keeping all other sources of uncertainty constant. This would allow the individual to determine reasonably conservative expected earnings of the company to allow investment.

Finally, the process would be repeated by varying the expected growth level to determine a reasonably conservative expected growth of the company to allow investment.

The individual would then combine all three scenarios of profitability, expected earnings, and expected growth of the company to make his or her final investment decision.

Similarly, following the example of Chapter 11.2, the resolution of uncertainties for the group decision process would be to consider creating and operating a professional association by varying the expected membership of the association while keeping all other sources of uncertainty unchanged. The group would then be able to determine a reasonably conservative membership level of the association to proceed with the decision to create and operate a professional association.

The above process would be repeated by varying the benefits provided to members, the political support level expected for the association, and the recognition or accreditation of the association.

The group would then combine all four conservative scenarios of association membership, benefits provided, political support, and recognition or accreditation of the association to make the final decision to create and operate the professional association.

12.0 THE IMMUTABLE ELEMENTS OF SUCCESS

It has been shown that the basis of the human behavior model includes varying factors, immutable factors, and other values and principles to guide and direct the individual towards task-oriented or relationship-oriented human behavior (Chapter 5).

This Chapter presents the immutable elements that will always support the individual in its successful behavior, regardless of other variable factors and values. These elements are not expected to change with time or space.

The immutable elements of success are the individual's

    (1) Knowledge
    (2) Integrity
    (3) Judgment
    (4) Interpretation and focus

The combination of knowledge and integrity is leading to the individual's credibility. There can be no credibility without the individual's knowledge and integrity.

The set of elements, knowledge and integrity that yield credibility, represents the cornerstone of any meaningful relationship between individuals, individual and group, and between groups. Credibility is an essential element for building trust which represents another element for confident relationship between parties.

Knowledge without integrity leads to a display of expertise and know-how that is part of a deceitful process since the expertise is being used for dishonest and untruthful purposes. As a result, the system to which knowledge without integrity is applied becomes untruthful and corrupt. The individual, or group of individuals, loses credibility and cannot be trusted.

Conversely, integrity without knowledge leads to a display of honesty and even probity that is part of a process without knowledge and substance. As a result, the system to which integrity without knowledge is applied becomes minor and inconsequential. The individual, or group of individuals, loses credibility since no knowledge is being used in the relationship.

Furthermore, the combination of credibility and judgment leads to efficient management.

Finally, management when combined with interpretation and focus yields successful leadership.

The immutable elements of success are shown in Fig. 8.

13.0 THE ERROR PROCESS

The error process is mostly related to the individual and group decision processes presented in Chapter 11.1 and 11.2, respectively.

In the decision process model, the initial areas for decision making such as knowledge, factors, resources, forces, and constraints, may contain information and data that are not fully known or that have been assumed. Those may be incorrect, incomplete, or obsolete. Furthermore, the decision process includes uncertainties and "what-if" scenarios that may use information or assumptions that are invalid, inaccurate or incomplete. This chapter describes the error process where errors are identified and corrected so that the decision-making process used by the individual or group of individuals is accurate, complete, and up to date.

The error process consists of five steps that are:

(1) Identification of the error
    This step includes the discovery of the error and the important decision to be made: start the error correction process or ignore the error.
(2) Analysis of the error
    As the error is identified, this step is devoted to analyzing the error, the source of the error, and assessing the potential impact of the error.
    In addition, the frequency and consequences of the error, hence the risk, caused by the error in the decision is determined.
(3) Judgment and interpretation

This step allows to judge the impact and the effect of the error, and the type of error involved. The interpretation provides further clarifications related to the error and allows to delineate the propagation and the limit of impact of the error.

(4) Corrective action

The corrective action involves a re-analysis, a verification, and ensuring that the decision process is error-proof. The applicable procedures are revised and the group members are retrained, as needed.

A report is issued summarizing the corrective action.

(5) Reporting

This step involves an important decision to be made with respect to reporting the error and its correction, and who the error should be reported to. Depending on the nature of the error and the severity of its impact, procedures should be used for reporting the error internally (i.e. to the group members or to the management of the organization) and/or externally (i.e. to users, customers, regulators, or other external organizations).

It should be noted that in all cases the internal reporting of the error should include its correction with lessons learned to ensure proper correction of the error and avoiding any repeat of a similar error.

A summary of the error process is shown in Fig. 9.

As an example of the error process applied to the individual decision process presented in Chapter 11.1, two errors may have occurred in the original investment analysis where the individual decision maker overestimated the growth of the economy (unleveraged force) and overestimated the growth of the company (resolution of uncertainty).

As a first step, the individual would consider correcting the error since the investment involves a sizable amount of money. The individual would also uphold any future investment in the company.

The second step would consist of analyzing the error and determining if the error resulted in a significant loss of the initial investment.

The third step would involve the review of the estimate of the growth of the economy and the growth of the company. This step would allow the sensitivity of the investment to the percentage growth of the economy and the company.

The fourth step would include a re-analysis and verification to determine the amount to be invested using the revised growth rate of the economy and the company.

The fifth step would include the reporting of the error and the revised analysis.

As an example of the error process applied to the group decision process presented in Chapter 11.2, an error may have occurred in the decision analysis related to creating and operating a professional association. The error may have been due to the overestimation of the support of the industry to the professional association.

As a first step, the group would consider correcting the error since the financial support from the industry may be vital for the creation and operation of the professional association.

The second step would involve analyzing the error to determine if the error in the expected support from the industry results in a significant shortfall in the initial investment needed for the association.

The third step would involve estimating the sensitivity of the feasibility to create and operate the association to the financial support level from the industry.

The fourth step involves a reanalysis and verification to determine the minimum level of financial support from the industry to allow the creation and operation of the professional association.

The fifth step includes a reporting of the error and the revised analysis. The reporting would be for group members and industry investors.

14. RISK METHODOLOGY

14.1 RISK RELATED TO HUMAN BEHAVIOR

The individual behavior model presented in chapter 3.0 allows the representation of the individual as a vector with a clear direction (the goal of the individual) and a magnitude that depends on components such as factors, values, resources, limitations, experience, and a multitude of unleveraged and leveraged forces (Fig. 2(a)). As a result, any uncertainty in the components of the individual behavior vector may affect the individual behavior itself. The question that arises is then the following: is the individual behavior vector going to be impacted by the uncertainties and, if yes, is the risk on the individual's behavior (magnitude and goal) acceptable?

Similarly, the group representation as a vector (Fig. 2(b)) includes a clear direction (the goal of the group) and a magnitude that depends on factors, forces, values, resources, experience, resources, synergy, and limitations. As a result, any uncertainty in the components of the group behavior vector may affect the group behavior. It is therefore important to determine the risk on the group behavior.

A rigorous risk methodology related to the individual and group behavior is not in the scope of the current effort for understanding human behavior. However, two methods may be recommended to estimate the risk.

(1) The first method is semi-quantitative and includes establishing permissible threshold values for the different components affecting the direction and magnitude of the individual (or group)

36

behavior vector. For a particular situation, therefore, the risk on the individual (or group) would be determined by considering the ratios of the different actual components and their threshold values. If the sum of the ratios is smaller than unity, the risk on the individual (or group) behavior, in terms of goal and magnitude, would be acceptable.

(2) The second method is quantitative and consists of weighing the different components impacting the direction and magnitude of the individual (or group) behavior vector. This would be followed by performing a risk analysis to determine the risk associated with each component, and the convoluted risk of all combined components on the individual (or group) behavior.

14.2 RISK RELATED TO THE DECISION PROCESS

The decision processes for the individual and for the group described in Chapters 11.1 and 11.2, respectively, include important steps where uncertainties may arise and impact the decision that is reached. The major areas of uncertainties are

(1) The knowledge, facts, and factors gathered
(2) The internal and external resources used and their verification and validation
(3) The forces and constraints exerted to ensure that all have been properly considered

Furthermore, following identification of the uncertainties, the decision maker must qualitatively

(1) resolve the uncertainties and determine their impact on the decision
(2) research and resolve "what-if" scenarios where uncertainties may be compounded as they impact the final decision
(3) determine the risks associated with the uncertainties considered in steps (1) and (2) above

The risk analysis related to the group decision is expected to be more complex than the risk analysis for the individual since the group decision process involves additional steps such as inclusion of subgroups, committees, decision review, and voting.

15.0 APPLICATIONS
OF THE MODEL

15.1 APPLICATIONS OF THE METHODOLOGY

The human behavior model presented in this report can be used for every individual and group. More particularly, the decision methodology described in Chapter 11.0 can be used for specific situations of individuals and groups facing important decisions regarding task-oriented or relationship-oriented processes where the proper behavior must be adopted to achieve the goals that were set.

As was seen, the important steps related to the decision process for the individual and the group can be summarized as the collection and analysis of facts and data, the identification of internal/external resources, the analysis of the decision to be made in light of forces, factors, and constraints, and the review/resolutions of uncertainties and "what-if" scenarios.

Illustrative application results of the individual decision process using the proposed methodology are presented in Tables 8 and 9.

The applications are: Application of Individual to Medical School (Table 8)
Adoption of a Child (Table 9)

Similarly, illustrative application results of the group decision process are shown in Tables 10 and 11.

The applications are: Creation and Operation of a Financial Investment
Company
(Table 10)

Creation and Operation of a Political Action Committee
(PAC) (Table 11)

Note that in each case the path to the decision is determined as

(1) the decision making includes the two-step process leading to a
final decision
(2) the risks and rewards of the specific situation are fully identified
and considered in the decision

For the sake of completeness, a contingency plan is provided, as appropriate,
after the final decision is made.

In addition, as discussed in Chapter 4.1, an example of vectorial operation
applied to potential spouses or partners is shown in Table 12. Individual
behavior vectors have been drawn for two individuals based on their values,
factors, forces, resources, and experience. Furthermore, a vector evaluation
was performed to determine additive and subtractive vector components
of the resulting vector.

The vectorial evaluation allowed to determine areas of compatibility and
incompatibility between the potential partners.

The analysis results include an assessment of the magnitude and direction
of the resulting vector. The results show that the magnitude of the resulting
vector was negatively affected in several aspects, although some elements
of the two individuals had a positive impact. The direction of the resulting
vector remained unchanged.

It may therefore be concluded that the two individuals will have extreme
difficulties in forming a compatible and harmonious union or partnership.

15.2 EXTENSIONS OF THE MODEL

The vector-based method developed for modeling the human behavior for the individual and the group is a first attempt to represent mathematically the effects of exerted factors and forces to influence humans to adopt a certain behavior to accomplish their goals. These goals can be material, spiritual, professional, family-oriented, or others.

Suggestions to extend the current model are provided below.

1. The current model includes a two-dimensional vector representation of human behavior, namely direction and magnitude. Additional vector dimensions could be used for a more timely and refined behavior model such as timeliness and sustainability.
Vectorial operations consisting only of addition and subtraction have been considered in the group behavior model. Other vectorial operations, such as vectorial product, could be considered in the proposed model for their possible behavior representation and effects.
2. Self-interest was found to represent an important leveraged force concentrated on the individual and the group itself for its own benefit. This force may be the dominant force in many circumstances as it may overwhelm many other factors, forces, and values. Self-interest and its possible dominance needs to be further investigated and integrated in the proposed human behavior model.
3. The error identification and correction process could be further refined and integrated into the model to allow an assessment of the decision process and human behavior on a regular basis and a correction of behavior, as needed.
4. A suitable computer simulation model could be developed to evaluate the individual behavior vector and the group behavior vector based on the input data related to the individual (Fig. 2(a)) and the group (Fig. 2(b)), respectively. These vectors would allow to determine if the individual behavior or the group behavior are adequate for the goals set.

Similarly, a computer simulation model could be developed to analyze and quantify the factors, forces, values, and other components impacting the individual and group behavior (Fig. 4(a)) and (Fig. 4(b)).

5. A computer simulation model would be needed to refine the individual and group decision processes (Figs. 6 and 7) to include more detailed input data and a more elaborate resolution of uncertainties having a direct impact on the individual and group decisions.

6. The risk methodology related to human behavior (Section 14.1) could be expanded to incorporate the uncertainties related to the individual and group factors, forces, values, and other components with direct impact on the individual and group behavior. Similarly, the risk related to the decision process (Section 14.2) could be expanded to include the uncertainties with direct impact on the individual and group decision processes.

7. The proposed human behavior model could be applied retroactively to historic personalities (such as statesmen, political leaders, etc.) and political groups (such as political parties, groups, movements, etc.) to understand and explain human behavior in light of historic factors, forces, constraints, resources, and other components. The historic decisions made could also be better understood and explained. This process could ultimately include the development of a warning and protection process for governments and responsible organizations if it is found that some human behaviors and decisions adopted in history had adverse or subversive effects.

8. The application of the model proposed in item (7) above could be used to contemporary situations to better understand and explain human behavior and decisions adopted by individuals and groups.

15.3 PROPOSED FUTURE APPLICATIONS

The proposed future applications of the proposed human behavior model are summarized below

(1) The human behavior model presented can be used for every individual and group. To that effect, identification and weighing of the unleveraged and leveraged forces can provide information regarding behavior directed towards purposes and goals. Progress and accomplishments can be monitored. When setting up the individual behavior vector (Fig. 2(a)), the model can be used to predict the probability of reaching goals. Positive and negative factors and forces need to be identified and monitored as they influence the direction of the behavior vector (goal) and the magnitude of the effort directed at the goal.

Continuous control of the leveraged forces and allocation of resources and experience are needed. Limitations on the individual must always be considered.

2. It was shown that an interesting application of the model is that it can be used to develop individual behavior vectors for two individuals who wish to marry and/ or live together. Based on the values, factors, forces, resources, and experience of the two individuals, the directions and magnitudes of the behavior vectors can be determined and criteria can be developed for compatibility and harmony. If the vectors of the two partners are found adequately aligned and compatible (in terms of direction and magnitude) the couple members may be found suitable for a harmonious union or partnership.

The preliminary model proposed could be further refined by adding more components to the behavioral vectors and quantifying the vector components to more accurately model the magnitude of the behavioral vectors of the two individuals.

3. The model proposed can be applied to set up a group behavior vector [Fig. 2(b)]. This vector can help create a standard for the group member selection, education requirements, training programs, and other requirements. Ultimately, all individual behavior vectors need to be aligned with the standard group behavior vector so that the group members are in full conformance with the group goals and requirements.

4. Varying and immutable factors, forces, and values need to be determined to assess the human behavior (Fig. 3). The role

of self-interest needs to be carefully accounted for, as it may overwhelm all other factors.

5. The unleveraged and leveraged forces exerted on the individual that have been identified (Fig. 4(a)) may be determined in any environment. As a result, the appropriate environment could be found or created to optimize human behavior.

6. The forces exerted on the group have been identified (Fig. 4(b)) and could be determined for any environment in order to optimize the group behavior. A difficulty may arise in determining the relative magnitude of the internal and external forces, as well as the effect of external relations on the group behavior. Self-interest of the group must be accounted for as it may represent a dominant behavior factor.

7. The effects of the unleveraged and leveraged forces and factors identified can be used in any vector-based human behavior model for the individual (Tables 2(a), 2(b), and 3(a)) and for the group (Table 3(b)).

8. The role of past experience has been identified and can be used to discern between meaningful experience and experience without impact on behavior.

9. The immutable elements of success have been identified to be used for management and leadership (Fig. 8).

16.0 CONCLUSIONS

The current work has been focused on modeling and simulating human behavior for the individual and the group of individuals. To that effect, a qualitative model has been developed to identify the individual subjected to factors and forces to adopt a certain behavior to accomplish his or her goals. Such goals can be material, spiritual, professional, family-oriented, and others.

A specific example of an individual submitted to unleveraged and leveraged forces was considered (Chapter 2.0).

Moreover, it was shown that the individual behavior can be represented mathematically by a vector with a specific magnitude (factors and forces) and direction (goal and purpose).

The vector representation was found adequate for modeling several influential aspects of an individual's behavior (Chapter 3.0).

The model was further extended to represent the group behavior as a vector. Examples of group standards that are used to sustain the group vector in direction and magnitude were identified. Characteristics of homogeneous and heterogeneous group vectors were provided. Particular cases for group vectors with respect to absence of magnitude and direction were discussed (Chapter 4.0).

The human behavior model was presented where it was shown that the various factors, values, self-interest, and limitations are exerted. They influence the individual to behave in a task-oriented or relationship-oriented environment (Chapter 5).

Many types of forces that may be exerted on the individual were identified (Table 1). These forces were identified as unleveraged and leveraged forces (Section 6.1). Unleveraged forces were defined as forces exerted on the individual regardless of the individual's will and interests. Leveraged forces were defined as forces due to the individual's will and choice. Furthermore, the effects of these forces on the individual were described (Sections 6.2 and 6.3).

Examples of factors affecting the individual's behavior were identified. These factors were found to include mostly laws, specific requirements on the individual, and factors affecting personal values (Table 3(a)).

Similarly, the forces exerted on the group were found to be based on the unleveraged and leveraged forces exerted on the individual (Chapter 7.0). Major differences exist, however, as the group behavior is more prone to be influenced by forces involving ideology, indoctrination, training of group members, and groupthink. Other differences were found to include internal and external forces and forces due to relations with other groups.

Examples of factors affecting the group's behavior were provided. These factors include mostly laws, specific requirements on the group, and internal and external factors (Table 3(b)).

The role of past experience in the human behavior model was defined and includes varying factors, immutable factors, values and principles, and self-interest that are exerted on the individual with a net result to influence him or her to behave in a task-oriented or relationship-oriented environment (Chapter 8.0). Past experience was found to include five distinct steps which are knowledge, analysis, learning and assessment, judgment, and interpretation.

Unleveraged and leveraged resources supporting the individual behavior in order to achieve his or her goals have been identified (Chapter 9.0). Similarly, resources supporting the group of individuals that include more group-specific means available to the group have been provided (Chapter 10.0).

A decision process that is part of the human behavior model was developed for the individual and for the group and was presented in Sections 11.1 and 11.2, respectively.

The individual decision process was found to rely on knowledge of facts, internal and external resources, forces, and constraints. The process also includes the resolution of uncertainties and "what-if" situations to reach a decision and adopt a behavior to act towards goals. This process was also found applicable to the group where, in addition, it had to include subgroups and committees for decision review, revisions (as needed), vote, policy, and decision implementation.

As a part of the human behavior model, immutable factors and values were identified to guide and direct the individual to act in a task-oriented or relationship-oriented environment. These factors and values, defined as the immutable elements of success include knowledge, integrity, judgment, interpretation, and focus (Chapter 12.0).

The decision process is further supported by an error process where errors are identified and corrected so that the decision-making process used by the individual or group is accurate, complete, and up-to-date. The error process was presented in Chapter 13.0 and includes five distinct steps that are error identification, error analysis, judgment and interpretation, reporting, and corrective action.

A risk methodology related to human behavior is presented where the uncertainties in the individual and group behavior factors, forces, resources, and limitations are discussed as they may impact the individual and group behavior (Section 14.1). In addition, the risk analysis is extended to the decision process to include the uncertainties and "what-if" situations identified to estimate the risk associated with the individual and group decision process (Section 14.2).

It was noted that the risk analysis for the group is expected to be more complex than that for the individual since the group includes more complex structures (such as subgroups, committees, etc.) and a more elaborate decision review process.

Illustrative applications of the individual decision process and the group decision process using the proposed methodology were presented (Chapter 15).

Several applications of the vector-based human behavior model were suggested (Chapter 15.0) such as

- Developing the individual behavior vector to predict the probability of reaching goals.

  The basis for such an application is the diagram shown in Fig. 2(a) and presented in Chapter 3.0. By using an appropriate weighting method to assign weights to the positive and negative factors and forces exerted on the individual and assigning weights to the direction of the individual's goal, one could determine and monitor the probability of the individual for reaching his or her goal.
- Developing the group behavior vector to determine the requirements needed for members to align their behavior with the expected group behavior and goals.

  This task would consist of constructing a standard group vector that would include all the requirements (forces and factors) and resources needed to focus on the group goals defined in Chapter 4.0. The standard group vector would then be used to "screen" the group applicants' vector for inclusion into the group.
- Identifying the unleveraged and leveraged forces exerted on the individual or the group to determine the environment for optimal behavior.

  After having identified the unleveraged and leveraged forces exerted on the individual (Figs. 4(a) and 4(b)) as was described in Chapters 6.0 and 7.0, respectively, the major contributors to the individual and group behavior vectors can be determined. As a result, one can recommend and make changes to the environmental system of forces, factors, and resources to optimize the behavior vector.
- Processing and filtering past experience to discern valuable experience.

  A process could be designed to filter past experience according to the steps presented in Chapter 8.0. This process would then analyze the facts and data and determine the impact of the experience on the individual or the group behavior. If the impact is positive, the behavior of the individual or group would be altered.

- Developing decision processes for the individual and the group.
  This task would use the processes described in Sections 11.1 and 11.2 for the individual and group decision process, respectively. The flowcharts shown in Figs. 6 and 7 could be used as a basis for computer simulation.
  The method presented in Section 11.3 may then be used for resolving uncertainties in the decisions with a reasonable level of conservatism.
- Identifying the immutable elements of success that could be used for management and leadership.
  The immutable elements of success presented in Chapter 12.0 may be applied to the individual to test his or her management skills and leadership. These elements are expected to be optimized to ensure that the individual will display a successful behavior of management and leadership, regardless of other factors and values.
- Developing an error identification and correction process.
  This task can use computer simulation to identify and analyze error(s) in the decision model and determine any impact on the individual or group decision process. The method presented in Chapter 13.0 may be used to that effect.

As a final note, human behavior modeling should be considered an evolutionary process since the model includes components and conditions such as factors, forces, constraints, limitations, and resources exerted on the individual (or group of individuals) that may vary with space and time. It is therefore recommended to update the variable conditions or components of the model to ensure that they are applicable to the behavioral situation considered.

17.0 REFERENCES

Cialdini, R.B.& Goldstein, N.J., (2004), Social influence: Compliance and conformity, Annual Review of Psychology, 55, 591-621.

Delre, S.A., Jager, W. & Janssen, M. (2006) Diffusion dynamics in small-world networks with heterogeneous consumers, Computational and Mathematical Organization Theory, 4, 5-22.

Jager, W. & Mosler, H-J, (2007), Simulating Human Behavior for Understanding and Managing Environmental Resource Use, Journal of Social Issues, Vol. 63, No. 1, pp 97-116.

Maslow, A.H. (1954), Motivation and personality, New York, USA: Harper and Row.

Max-Neef, M. (1992), Development and human needs. In P. Elkins & M.Max-Neef (Eds), Real-life economics; understanding wealth creation (pp.197-213), London, New York: Routledge.

Mosler, H-J & Bruchs, W. (2003), Integrating resource dilemma findings in a general dynamics model of cooperative behavior, European Journal of Social Psychology, 33, 119-133.

Rogers, E.M. (1995) Diffusion of innovations, Fourth edition, London: The Free Press.

Table 1. Types of Forces Exerted on the Individual

- Legal
- Economic
- Financial
- Fiscal
- Political
- Military
- Local
- National
- Social
- Managerial
- Professional
- Educational
- Scientific
- Artistic
- Musical
- Technological
- Progressive
- Vocational
- Divine
- Inspirational
- Religious
- Cultural
- Existential
- Safety-related
- Functional
- Communication-related
- Networking-related
- Health-related
- Sport-related
- Physical
- Fitness-related
- Natural
- Environmental
- Family-related

- Love-related
- Friendship-related
- Societal
- Spiritual
- Intellectual
- Self-motivated
- Self-Interest (Short-Term)
- Self-Interest (Long-Term)
- Peer-motivated
- External

Table 2(a) Effects of Unleveraged Forces on the Individual

Governmental:	Individual liberty, laws
Political:	Government policy, priorities, taxes, laws
Social:	Social values, status, hierarchy
Legal:	Individual liberty, justice system, laws
Natural/ Health related:	Laws of nature, Health of individual
Temporal:	Timing, time constraints
Environmental:	Structure, limits, laws

Table 2(b) Effects of Leveraged Forces on the Individual

Professional: Career, advancement
Ethical: Individual values, principles, code
Religious: Religious values, moral values, principles
Educational: Learning, knowledge, intellect
Economic/ Financial: Material and financial needs, financial situation, earnings, taxes
Technological: Technological needs, material well-being
Family: Values, support, influence, help
Self-Interest: All leveraged forces concentrated on the individual's self (Short-Term, Long-Term)

Table 3(a) Factors Affecting the Individual's Behavior

Laws
Financial / economic contracts
Education
Professional code and ethics
Natural and health requirements
Environmental requirements
Social requirements
Religious requirements
Personal values and principles
Family values
External influence
Self-Interest (Short-Term, Long-Term)

Table 3(b) Factors Affecting the Group's Behavior

Laws
Financial / Economic contracts
Professional code and ethics
Natural and health requirements
Environmental requirements
Social requirements
Religious requirements
Group values and principles
Doctrine/ Ideology
Pragmatism
Education
Training/ Indoctrination
Technology
Groupthink
Internal Factors (planning, organization, leadership, control)
External Factors (external influence, review, and control)
Relations with other groups (affiliation with other groups, common interests)
Self-Interest (Short-Term, Long-Term)

Table 4 Representative Resources Supporting the Individual

(1) **Unleveraged Resources**
Nature and health
Genetics
Character
Personality
Internal Resources

(2) **Leveraged Resources**
Family values
Education
Profession
Experience
Religion
Ethics
Values and Principles
Social Environment
External Resources

Table 5 Representative Resources Supporting the Group

(3) **Unleveraged Resources**
Natural
Character of Members
Personality of Members
Personal Values of Members
Social Network
Political network
Legal
Financial

(4) **Leveraged Resources**
Education of Members
Profession of Members
Experience of Members
Religion of Members
Ethics of Members
Group Values and Standards
External Resources
Indoctrination, Training of Members
Affiliations with other Groups
Internal Resources
Financial
Fundraising
Membership
Policy

Table 6 Examples of Applications of the Individual Decision Process
Methodology Applied to Specific Purposes and Situations

CATEGORY	PURPOSE/ SITUATION
Educational/Social	Pursue an artistic career
	Pursue a political sciences career
	Join an Ivy League school
	Join a fraternity or a sorority
Financial	Be an investor
	Make an investment
	Buy or sell a home
	Start own company/ business
Legal	Divorce
	Seek custody of a child
	Get married
	Live with a partner
	Seek to immigrate
Religious	Believe or not believe in God
	Convert to another faith
	Join a religious organization
	Pursue religious studies
	Seek ordination
	Join a religious cult
	Have a child baptized
Medical	Apply to medical school
	Pursue advanced medical studies
	Get a second opinion
	Undergo operation/ surgery

Family	Care for the elderly
	Care for a child
	Adopt a child
	Care legally and financially after a death in the family
	Join a senior association
Management	Join a management team
	Manage a project or a proposal
Academia	Pursue an academic career
	Join academia or remain a professional
Political	Join a political party
	Join a political organization
	Run for office
Military	Join the military
	Pursue a military career
Sports	Become a sports professional
	Promote/ manage a sports team
Professional / Employment	Remain with current employer
	Change job
	Quit a job
	Join a professional association
	Go back to college to earn a degree
	Accept a special assignment
	Retire

Table 7 Examples of Applications of the Group Decision Process
Methodology Applied to Specific Purposes and Situations

CATEGORY	PURPOSE/ SITUATION
Educational	Create and operate an academic organization
	Create and operate an artistic organization
Financial	Create and operate a business/ company
	Create and operate a start-up company
	Create and operate an investment organization
	Create and operate an organization of business professionals
Legal	Create, operate, and lead a legal rights movement
	Create operate, and lead a civil rights movement
	Join a bar association
	Join a jury
	Join a legal association
	Join a class action suite
Religious	Found a church or congregation
	Found a religious sect or a cult
Medical	Create and operate a medical organization
	Create and operate a medical specialty board
Professional	Create and operate a professional association
	Create and operate a private professional company
	Create and operate a professional consulting company
Political	Create and operate a political movement
	Create and operate a political action committee (PAC)

Create and operate a political party

Family   Create and operate a family association
Create and operate an association for seniors
Create and operate an association for children
Create and operate an association for immigrants

Management   Create and operate an association for financial managers
Create and operate an association for engineering managers
Create and operate an association for purchasing managers
Create and operate an association for marketing managers

Academia   Found a College or a University

Military   Conduct military operations

Sports   Create and operate a sports team
Create and operate a sports association

Arts   Create and operate an artist association
Create and operate a theater or dance group

Table 8 Example of Individual Decision Process:
Application of Individual to Medical School

Objective: Application of individual to Medical School

Knowledge/ Facts: Research medical school data, studies, curriculum, cost

Evidence: High competitiveness, time consuming studies, high cost

Risks: Not being admitted to medical school, not completing the MD degree requirements, not meeting the residency and Board Certification requirements, accumulating financial debt

Rewards: Being admitted to medical school, completing degree requirements, completing residency, meeting Board Certification requirements, owning a practice, being financially rewarded

Impact of Decision: High. Commitment to pursue studies for many years, no immediate financial reward, student loan debt.

Uncertainties: School admission, degree completion, specialty, residency, financial resources, practice location, Board Certification

Internal/ External Resources: Family, educators, friends

Evaluation of options: Apply to Medical School or explore other careers with more financial rewards, less risks

Initial Decision: Apply to Medical School

Factors/ Forces/ Constraints:

Unleveraged Forces: Time (time requirements of studies), regulation of medical profession, educational requirements, social requirements, benefits of profession, health requirements, legal requirements, economic/ financial requirements

Leveraged Forces: Educational and professional requirements, ethical requirements, technological requirements

Internal Forces: Set an educational and professional plan, control budget

External Forces: Peer pressure, family-exerted pressure

Constraints: Educational constraints, professional constraints, technological constraints

Immutable Factors: Personality, character, inner values, principles

Limitations: No physical, intellectual, or mental limitations
　　　　　Difficulty working with others. Applicant will work to improve interpersonal skills.

Self-Interest (short-term): Enroll in and complete a MD degree program

Self-Interest (long-term): Be a medical professional

Research/ Resolve Uncertainties: Apply to several Medical Schools
　　　　　Professional uncertainty
　　　　　Decide on medical specialty
　　　　　Complete degree requirements
　　　　　Meet medical residency requirements
　　　　　Apply for financial aid/ student loan
　　　　　Location of practice
　　　　　Meet medical Board Certification requirements

Final Decision: Apply to Medical School to become an MD

Contingency Plan: Apply to Graduate School for a degree in a scientific discipline

Table 9 Example of Individual Decision Process: Adoption of a Child

Objective: Adoption of a child

Knowledge/ Facts: Research child adoption data, adoption agencies, adoption market, adoption requirements, costs

Evidence: Difficult process, time-consuming, many requirements to meet, high costs

Risks: Not finding a suitable child to adopt, adoption requirements not met, child does not meet set of specifications, inefficient adoption agency, high costs

Risk (long-term): adopting a problem child (physically or mentally unfit), relationship with birth parents

Rewards: Parenting an adopted child, providing for a child's material and emotional needs

Impact of Decision: High. Commitment to provide for the child's material needs, care, and well-being for many years. Commitment to meet all child's financial needs.

Uncertainties: Ability to meet adoption requirements (physical, mental, and financial), search for the child, dealing with adoption agency, defining type of adoption, adoption costs, child's birth parents, child's physical and mental characteristics, child's character, child financial needs, child's special needs (if any)

Internal Resources: Family

External Resources: Adoption agency, friends who are foster parents or guardians Evaluation of options: Adopt a child or remain childless

Initial Decision: Adopt a child

Factors/ Forces/ Constraints:

Unleveraged Forces: Time (time is right for child adoption), government regulations, legal requirements, social responsibility, natural requirements (good physical and mental health of adoptive parents required), environmental requirement, financial requirement

Leveraged Forces: Professional requirement, ethical requirement, religious requirement, educational requirement, family-exerted force, peer pressure

Internal Forces: Set a parental plan, set a financial plan

External Forces: Family-exerted pressure

Constraints: Educational constraints, professional constraints, parental constraints, financial constraints

Immutable Factors: Demonstrated character, inner values, principles, personality, and social responsibility

Limitations: Applicant for adoption has no physical or mental limitations. Applicant has no experience with children. Applicant will learn to develop and apply parental skills.

Self-Interest (short-term): Being a parent. Providing for child's material and emotional needs

Self-Interest (long-term): Adoption of a child represents a fine addition to the family

Research/ Resolve Uncertainties: Meet all requirements for child adoption
Meet all financial requirements for adopting and raising a child
Complete study course for child adoption
Set accurate and complete specifications for child adoption
Work effectively with adoption agency

Select child, meet child, receive placement
Review adoption and other legal
documents
Change child's name
Set relationship/ contact specifications
with biological parents

Final Decision: Adopt a child

Contingency Plan: None

Table 10 Example of Group Decision Process: Creation
and Operation of a Financial Investment Company

Objective: Create and Operate a Financial Investment Company

Knowledge/ Facts: Research data on market and need for a financial investment company, data on investment products, data on customer needs, depositors, investors, data on competition, data on financial investment market

Evidence: Financial investment is lacking in geographic location of interest, there is currently no local market for financial investors

Risks: Difficulty building a financial investment team, structure of company is unknown, company must be appropriately capitalized (secure capital, depositors, loan, cost of capital), regulation requirements must be met, inherent risk in investment markets

Rewards: Acceptable investment and financial returns, lucrative markets, establish a solid business structure and financial team, build financial expertise within the company, offer a successful set of investment products to customers, minimize investment and market risk

Impact of Decision: High. Commitment to build a business team. Financial commitment to investors and creditors. Commitment to minimize time to make company profitable.

Special Tasks: Create a business plan, create a business investment team of financial experts, create a regulatory compliance team, create an oversight financial committee

Internal Resources: Company financial experts, investment officers, risk managers

External Resources: Financial contacts and networks, financial consultants, investors, regulators

Initial Decision: Create and operate a financial investment company

Factors/ Forces/ Constraints:

Unleveraged Forces: political, social, legal forces
Leveraged forces: Education, financial expertise, training, economic and financial forces, technological forces
Internal Forces: Planning, organization, leadership, financial control
External Forces: Relations with other financial investment companies, auditors, compliance officers, financial advisors
Constraints: Professional constraints, technological constraints

Relations with other Groups:
Relations with other investment companies, financial advisors, and investors

Self-Interest:
Short-term: Penetrate financial investment market
Long-term: Secure financial investment market share

Research/ Resolve Uncertainties:
> Economic conditions
> Financial and economic market conditions
> Difficulty securing investors and customers
> Financial investment competition
> Investment team and expertise
> Company capitalization
> Cost of capital
> Regulatory compliance requirements
> Investment risk
> Financial returns
> Competitive investment products (diverse, safe, timely)
> Length of time for company to be profitable
> Profit margin
> Unsuccessful investments and financial losses

Final Decision: Create and operate a financial investment company
Create a board of directors
Individual to act as chief investment officer

Contingency Plan: None

Table 11 Example of Group Decision Process: Create
and Operate a Political Action Committee (PAC)

Objective: Create and Operate a Political Action Committee (PAC)

Knowledge/ Facts: Research and collect data on current political committees and need for a specific PAC to address and support political issues (such as abortion rights, civil rights, voting rights, special interest organization such as NRA, foreign aid, etc.) and political candidates. Collect data on support for political issues and candidates in U.S. Congress. Collect data on political parties and officials opposing the issues, political candidates, and PACs. Gather facts on the issues from the executive, legislative, and judicial branches of government. Define the mission of the PAC in light of the political situation.

Evidence: Public interest on the issues is very high. A PAC is needed for supporting the political issues and political candidates for election at the local, state, and federal levels

Risks: Difficulty building a PAC to support the specific issues and candidates. PAC fundraising capability and capitalization are unknown. PAC capitalization needs fundraising and donor's network. All election commission regulations must be met. Inherent risk related to political campaign budgeting including operating income (fundraising, donors, etc.) and expenditures to support political issues (media advertising, campaign administrative costs, etc.).

Rewards: PAC successful support for political issues and candidates. Election of supported candidates at all levels. Favorable votes on the legislations supporting the issues of interest.

Impact of Decision: High. Commitment to build a PAC to support specific political issues and the election of political candidates.

Special Tasks: Define a political strategy, create a political committee, create a financial committee, create a business plan, create a regulatory compliance team, create an oversight financial committee.

Internal Resources: PAC financial supporters, fundraising specialists, political experts, legal experts, volunteers.

External Resources: Current and former elected officials, political analysts and consultants, media experts, legal consultants, political campaign volunteers, financial sponsors (businesses, individual donors, etc.).

Initial Decision: Create and operate a PAC

Factors/ Forces/ Constraints:

Unleveraged Forces: temporal, political, social, legal
Leveraged forces: Ideological, pragmatic, religious, ethical, economic and financial, and technological forces, and procedure and training-related forces
Internal Forces: Planning, organization, leadership, control (political, legal, regulatory, financial)
External Forces: Relations with lobbying organizations, interest groups, current and former elected officials, political consultants, media specialists, legal experts, regulatory agencies, financial advisors
Constraints: Political, social, legal, ethical, and regulatory constraints

Relations with other Groups:
Relations with political groups, interest groups, PACS, and religious and social organizations

Self-Interest:
Short-term: Create and operate a PAC with strong political and financial foundation
Long-term: Legislation supporting PAC's political issues, election of supported political candidates at all levels

Research/ Resolve Uncertainties:
    Current political status of issues
    Diversity and complexity of issues
    Fundraising capabilities
    Capitalization and budgeting of PAC

Donor network (individuals, businesses, etc.)
Volunteer network
Campaign budgeting
Expenditures to support political issues and candidates
Regulatory compliance requirements
Political and legal complexity of issues
Political opponents and critics of PAC
Success of political campaigns

Final Decision: Create and operate a PAC
Create a board of directors
Individual to act as executive director

Contingency Plan: Create an organization to be affiliated with an existing PAC

Table 12 Example of Vectorial Operations Applied to Potential Partners

Objective: Determine areas of compatibility and incompatibility between potential partners

Individual #1:
Behavioral Vector Components:

Values: Integrity, honesty, judgment, leadership

Unleveraged Forces: Social pressure, natural (health issues), economic/financial

Leveraged Forces: Professional (entrepreneurial), ethical, non-religious, educational (advanced), peer pressured

Immutable Factors: Strong personality, authoritative, often displays non-compromising character

Resources: Financial wealth, social network

Experience: Vast professional experience

Individual #2:
Behavioral Vector Components:

Values: Integrity, honesty, non-judgment
Unleveraged Forces: Time constraint
Leveraged Forces: Professional (clerical), religious, education (limited), family-pressured

Immutable Factors: Character (sociable, passive)
Resources: Modest financial resource, strong family network

Experience: Limited professional experience

Expected areas of compatibility (additive vector components):

Values: Integrity, honesty
Leveraged forces: Professional
Immutable factors: Character (sociable, individual # 2)
Resources: Financial and social

Expected areas of incompatibility (subtractive vector components):

Values: Leadership
Unleveraged forces: Natural (health issues, individual #1)
Leveraged forces: Religious, educational
Immutable factors: Character

Analysis Results:

The direction of the resulting vector is not affected by either individual since both individuals wish to have a meaningful partnership.

The magnitude of the resulting vector is negatively affected by
- The values of the individuals: one individual has excessive leadership (individual # 1)
- The unleveraged forces: one individual has health issues (individual # 1)
- The leveraged forces: both individuals show incompatibility of religious beliefs and levels of education
- The immutable factor: one individual is authoritative and displays a non-compromising character (individual # 1)

Recommendation: The individuals considered will have extreme difficulties in forming a compatible and harmonious long-lasting union or partnership.

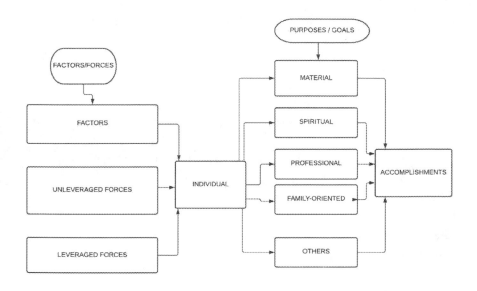

Fig. 1 Model of the Individual Submitted to Forces and Factors and Facing Purpose and Goals

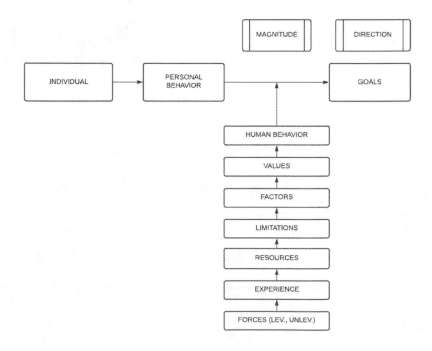

Fig. 2(a) The Individual Behavior as a Vector

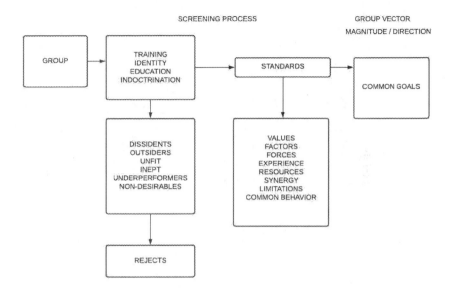

Fig. 2(b) The Group Behavior Representation as a Vector

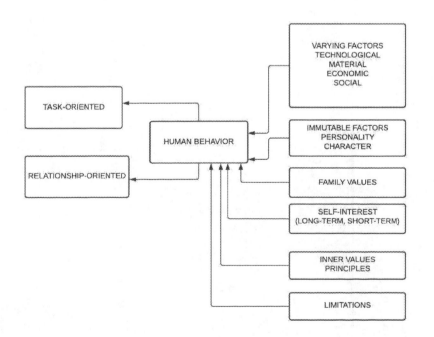

Fig. 3 The Human Behavior Model

77

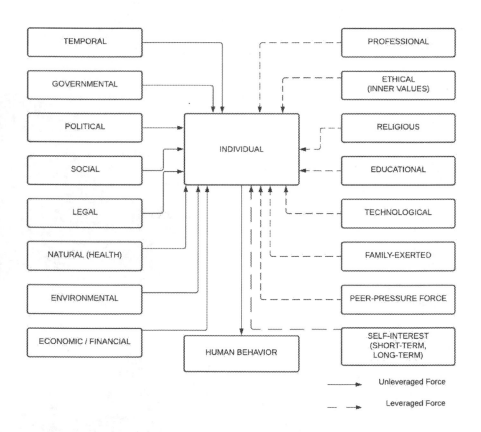

Fig. 4(a) Forces Exerted on the Individual

78

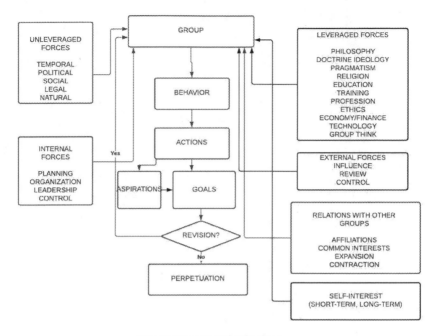

Fig. 4(b) Forces Exerted on the Group

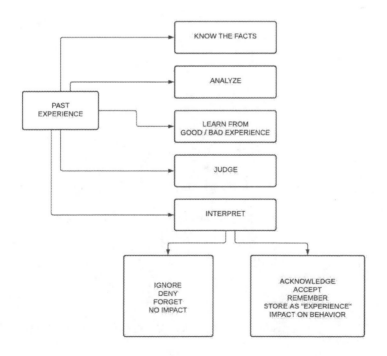

Fig. 5 The Role of Past Experience

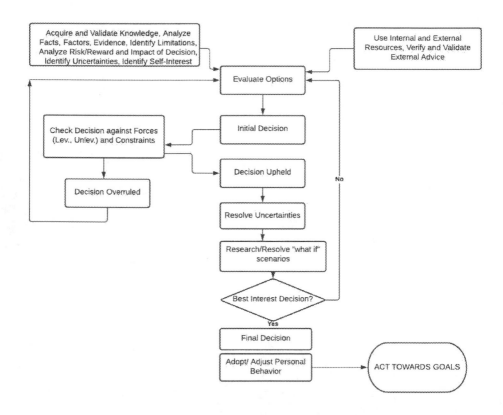

Fig. 6 The Individual Decision Process

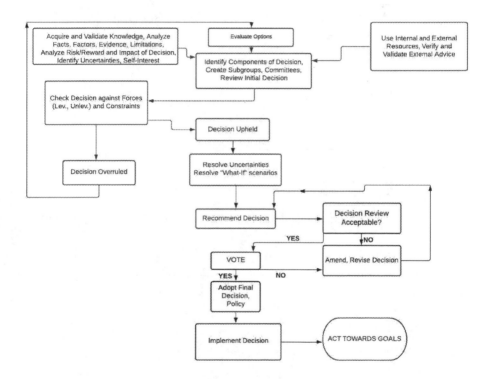

Fig. 7   The Group Decision Process

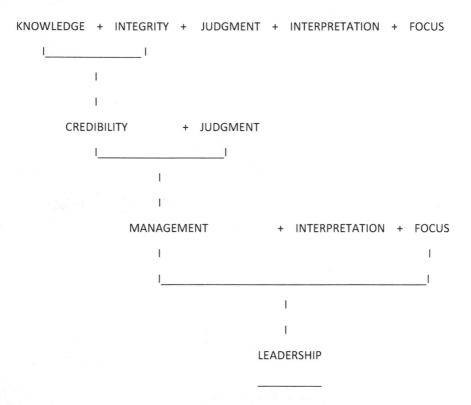

Fig. 8 The Immutable Elements of Success

Step I IDENTIFICATION	STEP II ANALYSIS	STEP III JUDGMENT AND INTERPRETATION		STEP IV CORRECTIVE ACTION	STEP V REPORTING
Discover	Analyze	Judge	Interpret	- Re-analyze	-Do not report
Recognize	-Source(s) of error	- Effects	- Impact	- Verify	- Report internally
Identify	- Inter-relationship	- Impact	- Limit of impact	- Error-proof	- Report externally (to regulators, etc.),
Categorize	- Potential impact	-Type of error		- Report	
	- Frequency			- Lessons learned	
	- Consequences			- Revise procedures	
	- Risk			- Training, as needed	
-Ignore	Consider				
- Deny	- Legal impact				
- Forget					

Fig. 9 The Error Process

Printed in the United States
by Baker & Taylor Publisher Services